Who the Great Molasses Flood of 1919?

by Kirsten Anderson

illustrated by Dede Putra

Penguin Workshop

PENGUIN WORKSHOP
An imprint of Penguin Random House LLC, New York

First published in the United States of America by Penguin Workshop,
an imprint of Penguin Random House LLC, New York, 2024

Visit us online at penguinrandomhouse.com.

Library of Congress Control Number: 2023039971

Printed in the United States of America

ISBN 9780593520772 (paperback)   10 9 8 7 6 5 4 3 2 1 WOR
ISBN 9780593520789 (library binding)   10 9 8 7 6 5 4 3 2 1 WOR

Contents

What Was the Great Molasses Flood of 1919?

January 15, 1919, was a warm day in Boston, Massachusetts—almost forty degrees by noon. That wouldn't count as "warm" in most places, but during the previous few days, temperatures had been close to zero. Near Boston Harbor, where there was a constant wind blowing in from the sea, it had seemed even colder.

That day may have felt like a short holiday from winter, but it was business as usual in the crowded area near the harbor. Ships and trains came and went, loading and unloading their cargo. Adults were hard at work. Kids went to school.

But then, everything changed.

At 12:41 p.m., Robert Johnson was standing on the deck of the *Bessie J.*, a US Navy ship anchored in Boston Harbor. Suddenly, he heard a loud rumbling sound from shore.

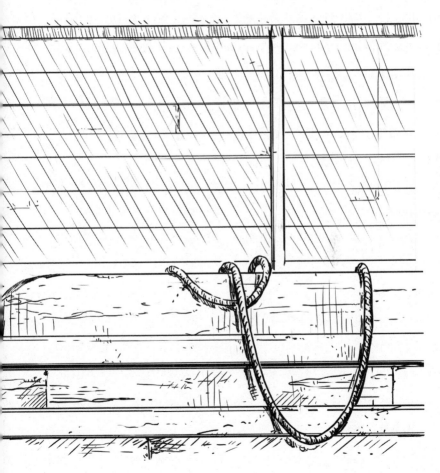

H. P. Palmer, an accountant, heard the rumbling from his office building near the harbor. As Palmer looked up, the entire building began to shake.

The firefighters at Engine 31 were playing cards and talking when they heard a booming crash. One of them ran to the window. "Oh my God," he shouted. "Run!"

Boston Police patrolman Frank McManus headed toward the callbox on Commercial Street. It was time for his regular check-in with police headquarters. As he began to call in his report, he heard a sound like shots fired from a gun. McManus turned around just in time to see the enormous molasses tank on Commercial Street collapse. As a wave of thick dark liquid rushed from it, the patrolman yelled into the phone, "Send all available rescue vehicles and personnel immediately—there's a wave of molasses coming down Commercial Street!"

It almost sounds silly at first. A monster wave of molasses oozing down a city street?

But there was nothing funny about the molasses flood. When the fifty-foot-high molasses tank burst apart that day, it released 2.5 million gallons of the sticky syrup, killing and injuring people and animals. The flood knocked down buildings and railroad tracks. It caused about $100 million (in today's money) worth of property damage.

What had gone wrong? And why was there a giant tank filled with molasses in one of the most crowded neighborhoods in the city of Boston?

CHAPTER 1
The North End

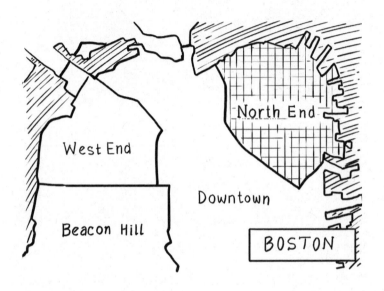

The North End is one of Boston's oldest neighborhoods, located right next to the busy harbor, where ships brought plenty of business to the area. There, the early English colonists had built wharves where ships from all over the world could dock, and warehouses to store their goods. Wealthy merchants kept offices near the harbor and lived in grand mansions nearby. By the middle of the 1700s, the North End had become one of the city's most fashionable neighborhoods.

That changed in the 1800s. The North End stayed busy. But there was so much noise and traffic that the people who had become rich from all the businesses there left for fancy new neighborhoods.

There was still a lot of activity around the docks. But the rest of the North End was neglected. Buildings fell apart. Trash piled up in the streets. It was no longer a safe part of the city. Many Bostonians stayed away from the North End.

But not everyone. In the 1820s, Irish immigrants began to move into the area. It was one of the few places they could afford to live. They packed into tenement houses in a small part of the North End. Tenements were larger old buildings that had been carved up into small apartments. Families crowded into one- or two-room apartments where disease spread quickly.

Tenement house in the North End

In time, many Irish immigrants settled into their lives in America and began to earn more money. They moved out of the North End and

Jewish people from Eastern Europe moved in. But they also left the North End tenements when they eventually became more successful. The next wave of immigrants came from Italy. By 1900, there were fourteen thousand Italian immigrants living in Boston's North End.

Like the Irish and Jewish people before them, the Italians faced discrimination. Just as they had been of the Irish, Americans were suspicious of their Catholic religion. Italians from places in southern Italy, like Sicily, faced racism because of their darker skin. Their food and its smells seemed strange to older, more established Bostonians. To them, the Italians just didn't seem "American enough."

Many Italian immigrants worked at jobs on the docks. They were laborers in the warehouses and the train yards. Others built small businesses in the neighborhood. They sold fruit from carts on the street or opened tailor shops or grocery stores.

There were Italian doctors, dentists, and banks in the North End.

Families were close. They learned to help each other with life in the United States. Women cared for each other's children. They leaned out their windows to share news with neighbors in the next building.

In 1910, about twenty-eight thousand Italian immigrants were living in the North End. They were packed into a residential area (where their homes were) that measured less than half a square mile. The commercial part of the neighborhood (where the industry and businesses were) was jam-packed, too. The city of Boston had buildings for stonecutters, carpenters, and blacksmiths. Carts pulled by horses squeezed past trucks with motors. Offices nearby were filled with employees. And the docks that had been busy for hundreds of years were still there. Several railroad lines crisscrossed around the docks, carrying goods in and out of

Boston. In the early 1900s, the Boston Elevated Railway Company had built trains on tracks that ran above the streets. Elevated trains rumbled over the busy North End all day.

It was one of the busiest, most crowded parts of the city. And in 1915, a business called United States Industrial Alcohol Company (USIA) decided it was the perfect place to build a giant molasses storage tank.

CHAPTER 2
A Rush to Build

Molasses is sweet, but it has a bitter history in the United States. Beginning in the early 1600s, molasses was a key part of the "triangular trade"—the path of the transatlantic slave trade. This route was shaped by the winds and currents between Europe, Africa, and the Americas.

So, what exactly *is* molasses? And why is it so important?

Molasses is a thick, dark syrup that comes from the sugar-making process. The plant that is raw sugarcane is crushed and boiled until it forms crystals. The crystals are sugar. The leftover syrup is molasses. The sugarcane crystals can be boiled again and again until they are white and there is no molasses left in them. That is the white sugar people use most often at home and add to coffee or tea. Brown sugar still has some molasses left in it. Although molasses can be found in popular recipes for cookies, candy, sweet breads, and pies, it can also be turned into a form of alcohol that's used to make alcoholic drinks and liquor, like rum.

The Triangular Trade

In the 1600s and 1700s, European and American ships regularly sailed to the west coast of Africa. They traded goods like cloth and rum for human beings, whom they enslaved. The enslaved African people were shipped to the American colonies and to the Caribbean. They were forced to work on plantations that grew sugarcane, tobacco, and cotton. Sugar, tobacco, and cotton were put onto ships and sent to Europe from the Americas, where they were sold and also used to make cloth and rum. Then the cycle began all over again.

Sugarcane

As the plantation system in the southern

colonies grew, New England ships began to sell enslaved people directly to those plantation owners. Disagreements over the issue of enslaving people eventually led to the US Civil War, and then to many long-standing inequalities for Black people in the United States. And molasses played a key role in that.

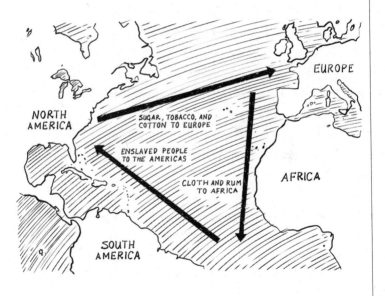

NORTH AMERICA

EUROPE

SUGAR, TOBACCO, AND COTTON TO EUROPE

ENSLAVED PEOPLE TO THE AMERICAS

CLOTH AND RUM TO AFRICA

AFRICA

SOUTH AMERICA

But alcohol made from molasses can be used in industry, too. By the late nineteenth century, cheap molasses alcohol was commonly used in cleaning products, dyes, and other materials. This was known as industrial alcohol. And this is the product the United States Industrial Alcohol Company specialized in.

There was yet another purpose for alcohol made from molasses: ammunition. Industrial  alcohol was used to make gunpowder. It helped guns shoot bullets and made bombs explode. And in 1915, guns and bombs were both very important.

By late 1915, the Great War, later known as World War I, had been raging in Europe for more than a year. The United States wasn't yet part of the war. President Woodrow Wilson told Americans that they would stay out of it, but many believed that the United States would eventually become involved in the fighting.

Some American businesses were already involved in the war in Europe. USIA was one of them. The company imported molasses from the West Indies, Puerto Rico, and Cuba to its factories and their molasses storage tanks in New York and Baltimore. They also had a factory for processing molasses into alcohol in East Cambridge, Massachusetts, near Boston.

The company knew they needed a storage tank in Boston to receive the molasses from ships and to store it for the East Cambridge factory. Arthur P. Jell was a treasurer at USIA. He kept track of the company's money. Jell was put in charge of building the Boston tank. It was very important to the company. Jell believed that if he did a good job,

Arthur P. Jell

he would get promoted to a more important position.

Arthur Jell found the perfect spot for the tank. It was close to the waterfront and the railroad.

Ships would be able to easily pump their cargo of molasses into the tank, and then it could be pumped out again into nearby railway cars that would take it to USIA's factory. The only people living in the area were the Italian immigrants, and Jell and USIA knew that they wouldn't complain about the tank being nearby. They didn't have any power in the city of Boston.

The land was owned by the Boston Elevated Railway Company. In January 1915, Jell began talks with the railway company about renting the land. But they didn't come to an agreement until late September, and USIA wouldn't be allowed to start work on the site until November 1.

This was a huge problem. USIA had a ship full of molasses scheduled to arrive in Boston Harbor on December 31. The tank needed to be ready in just two months. If it wasn't, the molasses might have to be dumped at sea. The company would lose money, and Jell's reputation would suffer.

World War I

World War I started as a conflict between the Austro-Hungarian Empire and Serbia. The dual monarchy of the countries Austria and Hungary controlled the country of Bosnia, where a number of Serbians lived. Many outside Serbians wanted to free the Bosnian Serbs so they could unite as one Serbian nation. On June 28, 1914, a Bosnian Serb named Gavrilo Princip decided to show the Austro-Hungarian emperor they were serious. He shot and killed the emperor's nephew, Archduke Ferdinand, and his wife while they were visiting Sarajevo, a city in Bosnia. The angry Austro-Hungarians declared war on Serbia on July 28.

The Austro-Hungarians had an agreement with Germany that they would help each other if one was attacked. The Serbians had a similar agreement with France and Great Britain. Soon, countries all over Europe had been dragged into the war. And in April 1917, so was the United States.

The war lasted until November 1918. Over eight million soldiers died. More than twenty million were injured. People called it the Great War because no one had ever seen such a big conflict. They also called it the War to End All Wars, because no one could imagine anyone starting another war like it. But they were wrong. In 1939, World War II began.

It took a month for the foundation of the tank to be built. At the beginning of December, the steel plates from the Hammond Iron Works arrived from Pennsylvania. Now they had to be riveted (fastened) together, piece by piece, to form the tank. Jell arranged to have men work night and day in order to finish in time. But storms shut down work a few times during the month. And Christmas was another lost day of work.

Finally, the last piece of steel was riveted into place on December 29. The finished tank stood fifty feet high from the ground to its roof—about five stories tall! It was even taller than the elevated railroad tracks, which were thirty feet above street level. The tank was ninety feet wide and measured 240 feet around.

In its contract, Hammond Iron Works had stated that USIA should first test the tank by filling it with water. But Jell knew it would take many days to pump millions of gallons of water into the tank. It would also cost money to get that much water from the city. Jell decided he didn't have the time or the money. Instead, he had the huge tank filled with just six inches of water! This was only a tiny fraction of the 2.5 million gallons it could hold when full. It didn't leak, and that was good enough for Jell.

A few days later, on December 31, 1915, a tanker ship full of molasses arrived in Boston

Harbor. The ship's crew pumped its liquid cargo into the tank.

Arthur Jell had met his deadline, and no money was lost for the company. His bosses at USIA would be very pleased with him.

CHAPTER 3
Warning Signs

Many Americans were unhappy about the possibility that the United States might join the war in Europe. There had already been bombings at factories that made weapons and ammunition, by people who were protesting the sort of manufacturing that supported the war. One such attack was in a suburb just outside Boston. These bombings were carried out by anarchists—people who didn't believe in government or capitalism (an economic system where private individuals own property and run businesses to earn profits). Anarchists were known to use violence to get attention and make their point.

The Boston Police Department considered the North End's Italian immigrant neighborhood to be the center of anarchist activity. USIA executives worried that their company could be another target for the anarchists. After all, the industrial alcohol USIA produced was being sold to companies that used it to fuel bombs and guns. And USIA was earning big profits from those sales. So they paid an officer from the Boston Police Department to stand watch over their tank near the harbor.

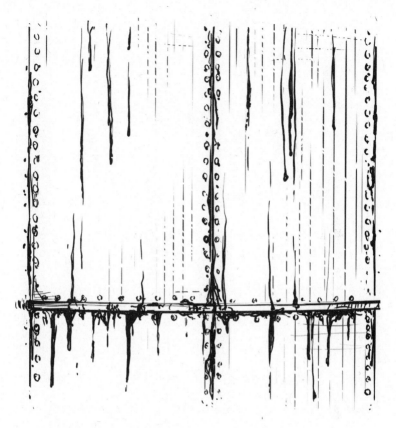

But the people who lived in the neighborhood saw other dangers in the tank. Everyone noticed the molasses dripping down its sides, where the steel plates had been riveted together. Kids even placed buckets under the tank to catch the sweet dripping molasses.

And the tank was making a strange sound. People near it reported hearing a rumbling sound coming from deep inside, like thunder trapped inside the steel tank. In June 1916, Jell hired a boilermaker—a steelworker who specialized in making tanks like this—to strengthen the seams where the tank's steel plates met. The boilermaker tried to push the plates closer together, to seal off leaks. But the tank was full, the work was difficult, and molasses kept dripping. Sounds like thunder kept coming from the tank.

Isaac Gonzales, who worked at the tank site for USIA, saw the leaks and heard the rumbling, too. His job was to check the pumps to make sure they were working, help ship crews pump molasses into the tank, and then help load it onto trains. Gonzales knew what was causing the sound. It meant the molasses was fermenting— the sugar was breaking down and turning into alcohol. In the process, the fermenting liquid released bubbles of carbon dioxide gas.

Gonzales worried about what might happen if the tank filled with the gas coming from the molasses. Would the pressure push the steel plates apart?

There were other problems. When Gonzales climbed into the tank to inspect it, flakes of steel fell onto his hair and shoulders. Was the tank falling apart? It made him nervous.

He told his boss, William White, about his worries, but White didn't seem concerned. Gonzales began to occasionally sleep near the tank. He thought that if it began to collapse, he would be close enough to warn other people about it.

Meanwhile, the United States entered World War I in April 1917. Now USIA was helping to make ammunition for American soldiers as well as European ones. Business boomed.

Later that spring, Isaac Gonzales went to see Arthur Jell at the USIA office in East Cambridge. He even brought some of the small bits of steel that had flaked off the tank. Jell simply replied, "The tank still stands—it will stand." He reminded Gonzales that the tank had been reinforced in 1916. And Jell told Gonzales to stop sleeping at the tank. That wasn't his job.

But Isaac Gonzales began to worry even more. Sometimes he woke up in the middle of the night and ran across the city to check on the tank. He wondered if USIA would ever repair it.

Finally, USIA did something. In the summer of 1918, a crew painted the outside of the tank dark brown. No one said why. But everyone knew. The brown paint was supposed to make the dripping molasses less noticeable. USIA wasn't fixing the tank's problems. They were just hiding them.

Soon after, Isaac Gonzales quit his job at USIA. He joined the army and went off to training camp in Ohio, leaving the tank far behind.

CHAPTER 4
The Last Molasses Delivery

On November 11, 1918, World War I ended. On the eleventh hour on the eleventh day of the eleventh month of the year, the countries involved in the war agreed to stop fighting.

For most people, this was good news. But executives at USIA were worried. The war had enabled their business to earn a lot of money. It might take time for businesses to go back to their regular use of alcohol made from molasses, like making cleaning products. USIA wanted to make sure the company stayed profitable.

They decided to focus on selling their alcohol to companies that made rum and other types of liquor.

But at the time, some people in the United States wanted the sale of alcoholic drinks to be banned. It seemed likely that selling and drinking alcohol would be against the law by 1920.

Arthur Jell ordered a big shipment of molasses near the end of 1918. He wanted to be sure that there was enough time for the USIA factory to sell its molasses alcohol before liquor sales were outlawed.

Prohibition

In the late 1800s and early 1900s, some Americans believed that drinking alcoholic beverages—especially in excess—was the cause of many domestic problems, including crime and poverty. They argued that alcohol should be illegal. And on January 17, 1920, they got their wish. On that day, the Eighteenth Amendment went into effect, banning the sale, manufacture, and transport of alcohol in the United States.

But plenty of people still wanted to drink and intended to continue. "Bootleggers" distributed alcohol, and sometimes smuggled it from other countries. Unmarked bars, or "speakeasies," allowed customers inside to drink if they knew the right password to say at the front door. Instead of making people less interested in drinking, in some ways Prohibition made it seem more exciting.

Although the US government ended up spending millions of dollars attempting to enforce the Eighteenth Amendment, it hadn't ended crime and poverty as people had hoped. Instead, some argued that Prohibition had made things worse.

On December 5, 1933, Prohibition ended, fourteen years after it began. A few weeks later, Americans welcomed 1934 with raised glasses of legal champagne.

SS *Miliero*

On Sunday morning, January 12, 1919, a boat called the *Miliero* arrived in Boston Harbor. The ship's crew began to pump six hundred thousand gallons of molasses into the USIA tank around noon that day. Temperatures were in the teens, but the molasses had stayed warm during the journey from the Caribbean and moved quickly through the pumps. By Monday morning, the *Miliero*'s crew was done with its work.

The Boston tank hadn't been empty when the *Miliero* arrived, though. It was already partially filled with molasses that had been there for weeks, getting thicker as the temperature outside dropped. When the new warm molasses struck the cold molasses, it began to ferment and turn from sugar to alcohol. The molasses churned and bubbled loudly. People near the tank heard the sounds, but they were used to them by now. No one thought much about it.

The tank now held 2.3 million gallons of molasses. It reached up to the forty-eight-foot, nine-inch mark of the fifty-foot tank. When the fermenting molasses created bubbles of gas, there wasn't much room left in the tank for them. The gas-filled bubbles began to push against the walls of the tank.

CHAPTER 5
The Wave

It was 12:30 in the afternoon on January 15, 1919, and Martin Clougherty was still asleep.

This was not unusual. Martin owned a bar and often didn't get home until 4:30 in the morning.

Before he went to sleep this day, though, he left a note for his sister, Teresa, asking her to wake him up at 12:30. Martin was meeting with his accountant to talk about selling his house on Commercial Street near the harbor and buying a new home outside Boston.

The Commercial Street house was comfortable, but Martin had grown tired of it. There were smells from the stables and slaughterhouses nearby. Noisy trains rumbled overhead. And that big molasses tank blocked all light from the house.

Martin lived with his mother, sister, and brother, plus a few boarders to help with the costs. Martin had worked hard and saved his money. Now he was ready to get his family out of the dirty, loud, and crowded neighborhood.

At about 12:40 p.m., Teresa came to wake Martin. Still half asleep, he began to get up. Then the house began to shake. Teresa yelled, "Something awful has happened to the tank!" and Martin blacked out.

When he came to, he felt liquid filling his nose and mouth. He was drowning. But not in water—in molasses! Desperate for air, Martin pushed his way through the cold sticky molasses and found himself being carried along by a wave of thick syrup. He grabbed onto something that looked like a raft. It was actually his bedframe. Martin looked around and saw pieces of his house floating everywhere. The powerful wave had knocked the entire house off its foundation and slammed it into the tall trestles that held up the elevated railroad tracks.

Martin spotted a hand reaching out of the molasses. He grabbed it and pulled. It was his sister. Martin dragged Teresa to safety. Then he went to look for his mother and brother.

At around the same time that Martin Clougherty was waking up, ten-year-old Maria Distasio was standing near the molasses tank. Her parents had sent her, along with her brother Antonio and friend Pasquale Iantosca, to pick up firewood. Some railway workers spotted them, and the boys ran away and hid. But the railway men caught Maria and began to yell at her.

As Antonio rushed over to help his sister, the men stopped yelling. They stared at something behind Maria. Then, the wave of molasses crashed over them.

Giuseppe Iantosca, Pasquale's father, was watching from the family's apartment. He could easily see Pasquale because of the boy's bright red sweater. When the wave hit, he watched in horror as the dot of red on the ground below disappeared into the dark syrup. Before he could even scream, the wave crashed into the Iantoscas' building and Giuseppe was knocked unconscious.

John Barry was a stonecutter who worked in the city's paving offices near the harbor, but as usual, he had gone to spend his lunch hour with his friends at the firehouse. The last thing he remembered was someone shouting "Run!" Now he heard some moaning from the other men. The force of the molasses tank had completely knocked down the firehouse and they were trapped underneath it. They were fighting to stay alive under the crushing wreckage of the building and above the flowing molasses. Pain shot through John Barry's entire body. He struggled to breathe, but a sticky substance filled his mouth and nose. He was lying face down in a pool of molasses.

When the molasses tank collapsed, it created a twenty-five-foot-high wave that was moving at thirty-five miles per hour. The wave of

molasses spread out in every direction, destroying everything in its path. It smashed buildings, cars, trucks, and carriages. It dragged people, horses, and every other creature down into the dark thick syrup and carried them through the streets or into the harbor. Pieces of the giant steel tank crashed down onto the streets, and rivets from its walls shot in every direction like bullets.

Royal Leeman, a brakeman on the northbound 12:35 Boston Elevated Railway train, looked out the window as his train rounded a turn. Suddenly the sky in front of him seemed to darken. The train shook and he heard a sound like steel ripping apart. Just behind him, the molasses wave had smashed into one of the trestles that held the tracks above the street. If his train had been even a minute late, it would have fallen through the gap that now pierced the tracks.

Leeman's train was safe, but he knew others were in danger. He crawled out of a window and ran up the tracks to North Station. He told the worker at the station to stop the southbound train coming from that station. Then he ran back south. He knew there was another train on the way. Trains can't stop quickly, so Leeman needed to get to it as soon as possible, long before the engineer would see the broken track. As the train approached, Leeman stood on the track, waving his arms and screaming, "Stop—the track is down! The track is down!" He knew the engineer couldn't hear him, but hoped that the message would get through.

And it did. The engineer slowly stopped the train, then got out. Leeman explained what had happened, then sat on the tracks, shaken. When he looked down, the whole neighborhood seemed to be gone, drowned by a river of molasses.

CHAPTER 6
Desperate Hours

Rescuers arrived on the scene quickly. Sailors from ships in the harbor came ashore to help, and firefighters and police officers rushed in from all over the city. Firefighters turned ladders into bridges, so they could crawl over the dangerous liquid without getting sucked into it. Others began to dig through the clutter of fallen buildings, looking for people trapped beneath the crush of beams and bricks.

Bridget Clougherty, Martin Clougherty's mother, was found in the wreckage of her house, killed when it crashed into the railroad trestle. Maria Distasio had died instantly as she stood near the tank when it collapsed. Maria's brother Antonio suffered a head injury but survived.

There was no sign of Pasquale Iantosca,
though. His father, Giuseppe, ran out of the
family's apartment as soon as he could to search

for his son. He looked everywhere, but the police blocked him from many areas. Giuseppe struggled to explain in English that he was looking for his son, a boy in a red sweater. But many of the busy rescuers didn't take the time to listen to him. After searching for hours, Giuseppe began to fear the worst.

At Engine 31, rescuers dug carefully through the firehouse wreckage. The second floor had collapsed onto the first, but the third floor still stood. If they weren't careful, the third floor might come down, too, and then there would be no hope for men like John Barry and firefighter Bill Connor, who were trying to stay alive. It was already too late for some. George Layhe, a marine engineer for the fireboats, had been trapped

George Layhe

under the firehouse pool table. The men around him heard his cries die out as he suffocated in a pocket of molasses.

Survivors were rushed to the Haymarket Relief Station, a branch of Boston City Hospital. Nothing could have prepared the doctors and nurses there for what they saw. Covered in dark molasses, the victims of the flood almost didn't seem human. Doctors and nurses had to work quickly to try to clean their patients off and rinse molasses out of their noses and mouths.

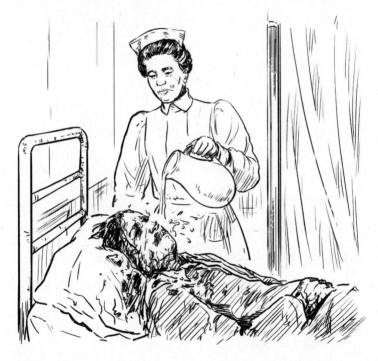

Before long, the halls and walls of the hospital were covered in molasses. Hospital workers mopped as fast as they could, trying to wash it away before it set and became stickier. When the injured were moved to beds, molasses continued to leak from their hair, noses, and mouths, leaving brown stains on the white sheets. Thirsty from the sickly sweetness that coated their throats, patients cried out for water.

Back in the North End, city officials had arrived on the scene. Boston mayor Andrew Peters stood in the lake of molasses and made a speech. He swore that an investigation into the cause of the flood would begin immediately.

Mayor Andrew Peters

Arthur Jell also came to the North End. William White, the tank supervisor, had called Jell to tell him about the disaster, and Jell had called his bosses at the USIA offices in New York.

They told him not to speak to anyone about the tank. Their lawyers would do all the talking. They asked Jell to go to the scene and make sure that no one took any of the pieces of the tank. USIA engineers would come the next day to get the giant steel plates.

Arthur Jell was stunned by what he saw. He could never have imagined anything this bad. He tried to approach the site where the tank had

stood, but rescuers told him to go away.

Henry F. R. Dolan, a lawyer for USIA, put out a statement. It said that the tank had been strong and could not have fallen by itself. Dolan wrote that "outside influences" must have caused the collapse. According to USIA, anarchists had probably put a bomb in their tank. The company did not believe that it was responsible for the disaster.

Time was an enemy of the rescuers working in the North End. The early afternoon darkness of January would make their search more difficult, but the nighttime chill would make it almost impossible. As temperatures dropped, the molasses would thicken and turn almost solid. Anyone trapped beneath it would have no chance.

John Barry made it. Rescuers worked for hours to free the stonecutter and firefighters Bill Connor and Nat Bowering. When Barry's daughters found their father at the hospital, one of them fainted. Not only was he covered in deep dark bruises, but his hair had also turned white. In a matter of hours, their strong, brown-haired father had turned into a broken old man.

By the end of the day, eleven people were confirmed dead. Many more were critically injured. Others were missing. The joy of a warm January day in Boston had turned into a nightmare for everyone in the North End.

CHAPTER 7
After the Flood

In the days after the flood, rescuers were replaced by cleanup crews. At first they tried to saw or chisel away the hardened molasses. That didn't work. The only thing that could dissolve the syrup was salt water pumped in from the harbor.

Boston city workers helped clear the wreckage.

The Boston Elevated Railway Company sent some of its workers. So did the company that had built the tank's concrete foundation. But USIA didn't send anyone to help with the cleanup effort.

Finally, on January 17, a vice president and engineers from USIA came to see the damage. An angry Boston city official scolded them for taking so long. He demanded that USIA help with the cleanup. USIA reluctantly agreed to supply 150 workers. They also began to remove pieces of their fallen tank.

Later that day, Ralph Martin, a truck driver, died of his injuries from the flood. Several more flood victims died at the hospital in the following days.

On January 20, rescuers found the body of a small boy. One of them remembered Giuseppe Iantosca, the man who had been looking for a boy wearing a red sweater. They brought Giuseppe to the site. The boy had been crushed by a railroad car and was almost unrecognizable. But Giuseppe knew that red sweater. It was ten-year-old Pasquale. Giuseppe tried not to cry in front of the rescuers. Instead, he prayed that his son had not suffered too much. Flaminio Gallerani's body was spotted in the harbor on January 26. He and his delivery truck had been swept into the harbor by the molasses wave. Gallerani was the nineteenth person killed by the flood.

For weeks, Boston investigators questioned people about the tank and the flood. In February, the district attorney presented evidence to a grand jury. They would decide whether USIA would be charged with a crime for building an unsafe tank.

The grand jury agreed that the tank had been poorly built. But they couldn't say that USIA had committed a crime. There would be no criminal trial. And no one would be punished for the deaths and damage caused by the molasses flood.

In May 1919, the body of Cesare Nicolo, a wagon driver, was found in Boston Harbor. He was victim number twenty.

Martin Clougherty's brother, Stephen, had been dramatically changed by the flood and the loss of his mother. He had been a gentle, peaceful man who lived happily with his family. After the flood, he suffered from constant nightmares and often became violent. Martin and his sister, Teresa, could no longer take care of him. Stephen Clougherty was sent to a psychiatric hospital and died

8 MOS
NATIVE CO
GALWAY IRELAND
BRIDGET
CLOUGHERTY
DIED JAN.15.1919
STEPHEN A.
CLOUGHERTY
DIED DEC.10.1919
REST IN PEACE

CLOUGHERTY

there in December 1919.

Many people count Stephen Clougherty as the twenty-first person killed by the molasses flood. Over 150 others had suffered life-changing injuries. And there had been about a million dollars of property damage in the North End. The story of the flood was not over. Someone was going to have to pay.

The North End of Boston, 1913

Boston Harbor, 1919

Stacked sugar at a manufacturing plant in New York, 1936

An American molasses mug from the 1930s

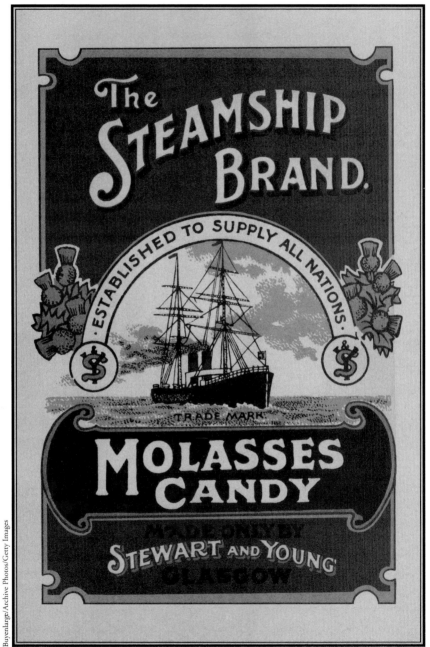

Packaging of molasses candy by Stewart and Young from the early 1900s

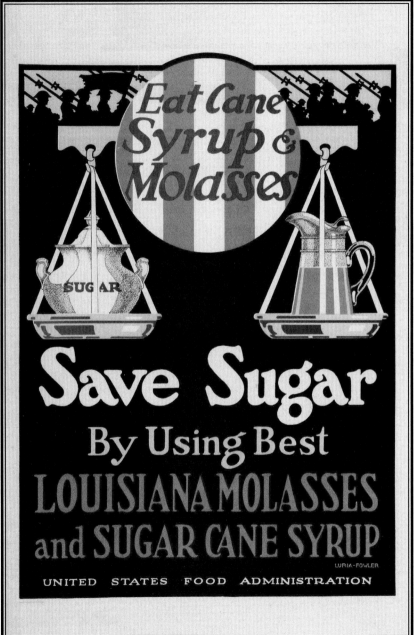

A 1918 US wartime advertisement for using molasses as a sugar substitute

A label for rhum vieux, an alcoholic drink made from sugarcane

Molasses being boiled in a factory in Saint Lucy, Barbados, in the 1890s

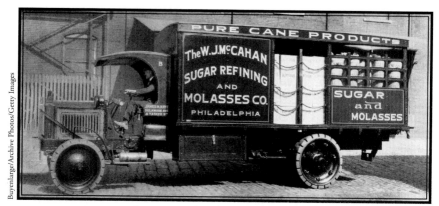

A sugar and molasses truck, 1900

New York City police pouring liquor into the sewer during Prohibition

Mayor of Boston from 1918 to 1921, Andrew Peters

People survey the ruins left by the molasses flood.

Commercial Street on January 16, 1919, the day after the molasses flood

Some of the damage caused by the molasses flood
in the North End of Boston

Police, firemen, Red Cross workers, and volunteers rush to the scene
of the molasses flood.

The remains of a fire station after the molasses flood

Welder cutting molasses tank with a torch to search for victims of the flood on January 20, 1919

One of the cars of the Boston Elevated Railway

Damage to elevated railroad tracks from the molasses flood

The one-hundredth anniversary of the molasses flood
remembered by Boston officials in 2019

CHAPTER 8
USIA's Defense

In the months following the flood, 119 people and businesses filed lawsuits against USIA. A judge in Boston Superior Court decided to put all the cases together into one lawsuit. Each side would have their case argued by one lead attorney.

Damon Hall represented the plaintiffs, or the people who had filed the lawsuits. Charles F. Choate Jr. represented USIA. Another attorney, Dudley Dorr, had filed one of the lawsuits against USIA after two of his buildings were destroyed by the flood. His name was put on the case, which became known as *Dorr v. United States Industrial Alcohol Company.*

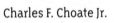

Charles F. Choate Jr.

The Boston judge took another important step. Since the case was so complicated, he appointed an "auditor" to listen to all the witnesses and review the evidence before the case even went to trial. The auditor would sort through all the evidence that was presented to him to find the most important information and arguments.

The auditor's report would make it easier for the jury if the case did go to trial. Hugh W. Ogden, a respected attorney and a World War I veteran, was named the auditor for the case. He was told the process would take about six weeks.

Hugh W. Ogden

Choate began arguing USIA's side of the case in September 1920. His goal was to convince Ogden that the tank was well built and could not have collapsed on its own. Choate wanted the auditor to think that an anarchist who was angry about USIA's role in the war bombed the tank.

Choate brought in many expert witnesses to explain why the tank could not possibly have collapsed on its own. Engineering professors from the Massachusetts Institute of Technology (MIT) and Harvard University said they believed that the tank had been fine. A steel expert spent three weeks explaining why the tank had been strong enough to hold the molasses. Chemists described how they had built smaller versions of the tank. They put explosives in these tanks and thought that they collapsed the same way as the real tank.

Walter Wedger, the state police chemist for Massachusetts, was one of USIA's most important witnesses. He did investigations for the state in cases involving fire and explosives. When Choate questioned him, Wedger stated firmly that he believed the tank disaster had been caused by an explosion.

Wedger seemed impressive at first. But then Hall, the plaintiffs' attorney, began to question him. He had Wedger explain that explosions usually shattered windows in nearby buildings, then got him to admit that no broken glass had been found near the molasses tank. Hall pointed out that Wedger had been part of the criminal investigation back in 1919, right after the

Damon Hall

flood. At that time, Wedger had told the court that fermentation from the mixture of cold and warm molasses had likely caused an explosion inside the tank. Hall asked him what had changed his mind. Wedger hesitated. Finally, he said that

he had only come up with his new opinion about the explosives after Choate, USIA's attorney, had suggested it to him. Hall made Wedger look unsure and confused. His report no longer seemed very impressive.

Choate's eyewitness to the tank collapse also didn't help much. Winnifred McNamara had lived across the street from the tank. She said that she had been on the roof of her building hanging laundry when she noticed smoke near the tank before it collapsed.

But McNamara struggled to answer Hall's questions. She couldn't say where exactly she had seen smoke. She also admitted that she never saw anyone suspicious near the tank.

Choate had finished his side of the case. He hoped he had made it clear that USIA was not responsible for the tank collapsing or any damages caused by it. Now it was up to Damon Hall to prove the opposite: USIA *was* to blame.

CHAPTER 9
The Plaintiffs' Case

Hall began to make his case in the late fall of 1920. He wanted to show Ogden that USIA had done a poor job building the tank, and then ignored the signs that it was failing. He believed USIA had known there was trouble, but the company only cared about keeping the tank running so they could make money during the war.

The first witness came from the Boston

Building Department. Clerk Josaphat Blain saw the plans that Hammond Iron Works had filed for the tank. They stated how thick the tank's steel plates were supposed to be. But now it had been found that the plates were thinner than what was in the original plans. USIA's lawyer Choate said it wasn't enough to weaken the tank. And professionals expected slight differences to happen when building things. Hall argued that it was still unacceptable. The walls of the tank should have been thicker.

Next Hall brought in witnesses who lived and worked around the tank. They described how the tank had started to leak almost immediately. Many witnesses noted how children would stand under the tank with pails to catch the steady drips of molasses. They explained how the tank seemed to shake and rumble when it was being filled. And everyone remembered how USIA had suddenly painted the tank dark brown. They all knew that it was done to make the leaking less noticeable.

Hall talked to Isaac Gonzales, too. The former USIA employee told the court about his visit to Arthur Jell at USIA's office to warn him that the tank was dangerous, and how Jell hadn't been interested in what he had to say. Hall also questioned the men who had been brought in to try to patch the leaks in the tank. They said the job had been difficult because the tank had so many leaks.

Then Hall brought in a group of soldiers who had been on ships in Boston Harbor on the day of the flood. They had spent the war working with explosives. Hall asked them if they had heard or seen anything before the tank collapse that made them think a bomb had gone off. They said they had not. They knew what exploding bombs sounded like. And they did not hear that sound on January 15, 1919.

Hall's most important witness was Arthur Jell himself. Jell now worked in USIA's New York office. But the company tried everything they could think of to keep him from appearing in court. They said he wasn't really part of this case.

The judge disagreed and said he had to be questioned by the attorneys. Then USIA said Jell couldn't travel to Boston to appear in court. Finally, they agreed to let Jell be interviewed in New York. In March 1921, Hall, Choate, Dolan, and a court reporter met Jell in a New York hotel.

Damon Hall asked Arthur Jell about his background. Jell explained that he worked in finance for USIA. He did not have a background in construction or architecture. He did not know how to read building plans. He just knew about

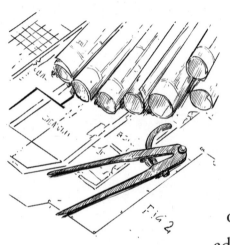

money. Then Hall got Jell to admit that he never had any experts look at the plans for the tank. He did not talk to any engineers or architects. He also admitted that he did not have any professionals inspect the steel plates when they arrived in Boston. He didn't have anyone examine the tank once it was built. And even though the contract for building the tank had recommended that USIA test it by filling it completely with water after it was built, Jell had only tested the tank by filling it with six inches of water. When asked why, Jell said that the real test would take too much time and cost money. His testimony worked against USIA. It showed a man, and a company, who were more concerned with time and money than building the tank safely.

Hall finished his case. He and Choate had been focused on proving who was at fault for the flood. Now Ogden wanted to hear how the flood had affected the people suing USIA.

For two years, Ogden listened to all their stories. Martin Clougherty told him that he still had nightmares about the flood. His sister, Teresa, said she was scared to leave their new home outside Boston. John Barry, the stonecutter, described the constant pain he felt from his injuries. Giuseppe Iantosca talked about watching his son Pasquale get swallowed up by the giant molasses wave.

After that, Choate and Hall spent eleven weeks making their closing arguments. Then they all waited for the judge's decision.

CHAPTER 10
Blame and Money

On April 28, 1925, Hugh Ogden, the auditor for *Dorr v. USIA Company*, was ready to state his opinion about the evidence he had reviewed. It had been more than six years since the molasses flood disaster in the North End.

Ogden wrote that he believed USIA was responsible for the collapse of the tank. He said that the company had not produced any evidence that a bomb had caused the tank to explode. There were no explosives found at the site. No mysterious person had been seen near the tank that day. And there wasn't any broken glass, a common clue in bombings. Based on the expert witnesses he had heard, Ogden believed that the tank had collapsed because it was poorly constructed. Even USIA's experts had said that the steel plates could have been stronger, although they still argued the tank was safe enough.

Ogden also felt that USIA had made a mistake by putting Arthur Jell, who knew nothing about building, in charge of the tank. The auditor blamed USIA for never testing or inspecting the tank. And he criticized the company for not taking any action when people like Isaac Gonzales warned them that the tank was breaking down.

Next, Ogden recommended amounts to be paid for damages to the plaintiffs in the lawsuit. His total came to about five million dollars in today's money. He suggested smaller amounts for the city of Boston and the Boston Elevated Railway Company for the damage to their buildings. Putting value on people's lives was more complicated. Ogden seemed to have thought that $6,000 was a starting point for the people killed in the flood. This was probably based on the idea that most of the dead had worked for the city or as laborers. They were not likely to have earned large amounts of money in their lifetime. Railway workers may have only made five to seven dollars per day. An unskilled laborer would have been paid twenty to forty cents per hour. That is not a fair way to value people's lives. But at the time it may have seemed like the best idea.

Ogden also considered how much a person may have suffered. He suggested that the families of those who were killed instantly, like Maria

Distasio and Bridget Clougherty, only receive $6,000 each. The family of George Layhe got a recommendation of $7,000. Layhe was the firefighter who slowly drowned under the firehouse pool table. Ogden offered $7,500 to the family of James McMullen, a railway worker who died after several agonizing days in the hospital.

The report also suggested amounts for people who had suffered injuries in the flood. John Barry, the stonecutter who spent hours waiting to be rescued, had a recommended amount of $4,000. Martin and Teresa Clougherty were offered $2,500 each, plus $1,800 for the house they had lost.

Damon Hall, the attorney for the plaintiffs, thought the amounts were not enough. He wanted to go to trial. There, the amount of damages would be decided by a jury.

USIA had had enough. The company feared that a sympathetic jury might recommend much more. USIA offered to negotiate the amount of damages privately. Within hours, they settled on an amount. The final total was more than eight million in today's dollars.

In time, the North End was rebuilt. But not the molasses tank. USIA had already closed its molasses processing factory in 1919, several months after the flood. Alcohol made from molasses was being replaced by other products. It was no longer a profitable business.

The North End in 1930

For decades, people said they could smell molasses in the North End on warm summer days. That's no longer true. The only reminder left of the flood is a small plaque near where the giant tank had once towered over Commercial Street.

But the flood did leave its mark in other ways. The city of Boston tightened its rules for constructing buildings. Engineers and architects had to sign off on plans they filed. A professional engineer had to put a seal on building plans before the city would give the builders a permit. Other cities and states created similar rules. Buildings became safer.

People sometimes say that something is "as slow as molasses in January." But anyone who has heard about the Boston molasses flood of 1919 knows that molasses isn't always slow. Sometimes it can be fast. And deadly.

Timeline of the Great Molasses Flood

1915 — United States Industrial Alcohol Company builds a new molasses tank in Boston under the supervision of Arthur Jell

1916 — USIA has the tank patched to try to stop the leaking

1917 — Isaac Gonzales visits Arthur Jell at his USIA office to warn him about the tank leaking

1918 — USIA paints the tank brown in August to hide the leaks

1919 — The molasses tank collapses, and molasses floods the North End on January 15, killing twenty-one people and injuring more than one hundred and fifty

1920 — 119 civil lawsuits against USIA are combined into one case, named *Dorr v. USIA Company*

— Attorneys begin arguing their cases before auditor Hugh Ogden in September

1921 — Jell is questioned by Damon Hall in March

— In July, attorneys finish arguing whether USIA is responsible for the tank collapse

1923 — On September 29, the molasses flood hearings end

1925 — Ogden states his opinion that USIA is responsible for the tank collapse

— USIA and the plaintiffs settle privately on a higher amount of damages to avoid a jury trial

Timeline of the World

1915 — German submarines sink the British ship *Lusitania*, killing 1,198 passengers and crew members

1916 — Jeannette Rankin of Montana becomes the first woman elected to serve in Congress

1917 — The United States enters World War I on April 6

1918 — The Spanish Flu pandemic begins, killing millions of people worldwide

1919 — The Treaty of Versailles, officially ending World War I, is signed in June

1920 — The Nineteenth Amendment is passed, giving American women the right to vote

1921 — The Tulsa Race Massacre takes place, with hundreds of Black Americans murdered and thousands imprisoned

1922 — The Tomb of Tutankhamen is discovered in Egypt by British archaeologist Howard Carter

1923 — The first home game is played in the original Yankee Stadium in New York City

1925 — F. Scott Fitzgerald's novel *The Great Gatsby* is published

Bibliography

Buell, Spencer. "Anarchists, Horses, Heroes: 12 Things You Didn't Know About the Great Boston Molasses Flood." *Boston*, January 12, 2019. https://www.bostonmagazine.com/news/2019/01/12/great-boston-molasses-flood-things-you-didnt-know/.

"The Great Molasses Disaster of 1919—A Strange Case in Boston Folklore." *Chambers Associate*. https://www.chambers-associate.com/where-to-start/commercial-awareness/regional-insights/boston-legal-history-the-great-molasses-disaster.

"The Great Molasses Flood." *Mass Moments*. https://www.massmoments.org/moment-details/great-molasses-flood.html.

"Italians." *Global Boston*. https://globalboston.bc.edu/index.php/home/ethnic-groups/italians/.

MacNeill, Arianna. "How Newspapers at the Time Covered the Great Molasses Flood." *Boston.com*, January 14, 2019. https://www.boston.com/news/history/2019/01/14/great-molasses-flood-newspapers/.

Nichols, Guild. "North End History—The Italians." *Pastene.com*, September 7, 2015. https://www.pastene.com/press/north-end-history-the-italians/.

Park, Edwards. "Without Warning, Molasses in January Surged Over Boston." *Smithsonian*, November 1983. https://edp.org/molpark.htm.

Press, Julia. "Remembering The Great Boston Molasses Flood, 100 Years Later." *Connecticut Public Radio*, January 10, 2019. https://www.ctpublic.org/arts-and-culture/2019-01-10/remembering-the-great-boston-molasses-flood-100-years-later.

Puleo, Stephen. *Dark Tide: The Great Molasses Flood of 1919*. Boston: Beacon Press, 2003.